FOOD LOVERS

BREADS AND MUFFINS

RECIPES SELECTED BY JONNIE LÉGER

Trans Atlantic Press

For best results when cooking the recipes in this book, buy fresh ingredients and follow the instructions carefully. Note that as a general rule vulnerable groups such as the very young, elderly people, pregnant women, convalescents and anyone suffering from an illness should avoid dishes that contain raw or lightly cooked eggs.

For all recipes, quantities are given in standard U.S. cups and imperial measures, followed by the metric equivalent. Follow one set or the other, but not a mixture of both because conversions may not be exact. Standard spoon and cup measurements are level and are based on the following:

1 tsp = 5 ml, 1 tbsp = 15 ml, 1 cup = 250 ml / 8 fl oz.

Note that Australian standard tablespoons are 20 ml, so Australian readers should use 3 tsp in place of 1 tbsp when measuring small quantities.

The electric oven temperatures in this book are given for conventional ovens with top and bottom heat. When using a fan oven, the temperature should be decreased by about 20–40ºF / 10–20ºC – check the oven manufacturer's instruction book for further guidance. The cooking times given should be used as an approximate guideline only.

Although the recipes in this book are believed to be accurate and true at the time of going to press, neither the authors nor the publisher can accept any legal responsibility or liability for any errors or omissions that may be made nor for any inaccuracies nor for any harm or injury that may come about from following instructions or advice given in this book.

CONTENTS

RED ONION FOCACCIA	4
CHERRY MUFFINS with CRUMBLE TOPPING	6
FARMHOUSE WHITE LOAF	8
POTATO and CHEESE MUFFINS	10
APPLE and CINNAMON MUFFINS	12
APPLE MUFFINS with SUNFLOWER SEEDS	14
CARROT BREAD	16
PINEAPPLE and CARROT MUFFINS	18
CRANBERRY BREAD	20
SOYA WHOLEMEAL BREAD	22
ROSEMARY BREAD	24
LEMON and POPPY SEED MUFFINS	26
BANANA, ZUCCHINI and APRICOT LOAF	28
PLUM and ALMOND MUFFINS	30
OAT and RAISIN BREAD	32
APPLE SCONES	34
WALNUT and RAISIN LOAF	36
CRANBERRY ROCK CAKES	38
BANANA and RAISIN MUFFINS	40
SODA BREAD	42
BLUEBERRY MUFFINS	44
PARMESAN and POLENTA MUFFINS	46

RED ONION FOCACCIA

Ingredients
Makes 8

4¼ cups / 425 g strong white bread flour

1 tsp salt

3 tbsp olive oil

1 tsp easy-blend dried yeast

1⅓ cups / 325 ml lukewarm water

1 red onion, sliced

1 lemon

Method
Prep and cook time: 40 min plus 30 min rising

1 Grease 2 large baking sheets. Put the flour and salt into a large bowl. Add 1 tbsp of the oil and sprinkle in the dried yeast.

2 Pour in the water and mix together with your hands until the mixture combines to make a ball.

3 Turn the dough out on to a lightly floured surface and knead for 10 minutes until smooth and elastic.

4 Divide the dough into 8 pieces and roll each piece into a ball with your hands. Using a rolling pin, roll each piece into a flattened round and put on to the prepared baking sheets.

5 Cover loosely with plastic wrap (clingfilm) or a clean tea towel and leave to rise in a warm place for about 30 minutes until doubled in size.

6 Meanwhile, heat 1 tbsp of the oil in a skillet (frying pan) and add the onion. Cook gently for 5 minutes until the onions are softened but not colored.

7 Either squeeze the lemon juice over the onions or cut the lemons into very thin slices.

8 Preheat the oven to 425°F (220°C / Gas Mark 7). Press a few indentations into the top of the bread with your finger. Arrange some lemon slices on top of each one, if using, and top with the onions. Drizzle over the remaining oil.

9 Bake in the oven for 20 minutes until golden brown. The bread is cooked when the base is tapped and it sounds hollow. Leave to cool on a wire rack.

CHERRY MUFFINS WITH CRUMBLE TOPPING

Ingredients

Makes 12

6 tbsp / 90 g butter

3½ cups / 350 g all purpose (plain) flour

4 tsp baking powder

1 cup / 200 g superfine (caster) sugar

Finely grated zest 1 lemon

5 oz / 150 g pitted sweet fresh or frozen cherries

2 eggs

1 cup /250 ml milk

¾ cup / 175 g cream cheese

¼ cup / 25 g ground almonds

Method

Prep and cook time: 45 min

1 Preheat the oven to 400°F (200°C / Gas Mark 6). Line a 12 hole muffin pan with paper muffin cases.

2 Melt 5 tbsp / 75 g the butter. Sift the flour and baking powder into a large bowl. Add a heaped ½ cup / 125 g of sugar, the lemon zest and the cherries. Stir together to coat the cherries in the flour.

3 Put the eggs and melted butter in a jug and mix together with a fork.

4 Add the liquid ingredients to the flour mixture and stir together until just combined.

5 Melt the remaining butter and set aside.

6 Put the cream cheese in a bowl and mix in 2 tbsp of sugar.

7 Divide half the muffin mixture equally between the muffin cases. Spoon a dollop of cream cheese into each one. Top with the remaining muffin mixture.

8 Add the remaining sugar and the ground almonds to the remaining melted butter and mix together. Sprinkle the crumble mixture over the top of each muffin.

9 Bake in the oven for 15 minutes until the muffins are well risen and firm. Leave to cool on a wire rack.

FARMHOUSE WHITE LOAF

Ingredients
Makes 1 loaf

5 cups / 500 g strong white bread flour

1 tbsp superfine (caster) sugar

1½ tsp salt

1 tsp easy-blend dried yeast

2 tbsp milk powder

4 tbsp / 50 g butter

1½ cups / 350 ml lukewarm water

Method
Prep and cook time: 50 min plus 1 hour rising

1 Grease a 2 lb / 900 g loaf pan (tin). Put the flour, sugar and salt into a large bowl. Sprinkle over the dried yeast and milk powder.

2 Add the butter in small pieces and pour in the warm water. Bring the mixture together with your hands to make a rough ball.

3 Turn the dough out on to a lightly floured surface and knead for 10 minutes until smooth and elastic.

4 Cover loosely with plastic wrap (clingfilm) or a clean tea towel and leave to rise in a warm place for about 30 minutes until doubled in size.

5 Knock back the dough on a lightly floured surface and knead for a few minutes. Shape into a rectangle. Put the dough into the prepared loaf pan.

6 Cover with a clean tea towel and leave for a further 30 minutes until the dough has risen to the top of the pan.

7 Preheat the oven to 400°F (200°C / Gas Mark 6). Bake the bread in the oven for 35 minutes until golden brown. The bread is cooked when the base is tapped and it sounds hollow. Leave to cool on a wire rack.

POTATO AND CHEESE MUFFINS

Ingredients
Makes 12

4 oz / 125 g potato

6 tbsp / 75 g butter

1½ cups / 150 g all purpose (plain) flour

¾ cup / 100 g cornstarch (cornflour)

1 tbsp baking powder

½ tsp salt

1 tbsp sugar

1 tsp fresh thyme leaves

1 cup / 225 ml milk

1 egg

1½ oz / 40 g Swiss (Gruyère) cheese, plus extra to serve

12 watercress sprigs, to garnish

Tomato salsa, to serve

Method
Prep and cook time: 40 min

1 Cut the potato into small cubes, put in a pan, cover with salted water and bring to the boil. Simmer for 10 minutes until almost tender.

2 Preheat the oven to 200°C (400°F / Gas Mark 6). Grease a 12 hole muffin pan or line with paper muffin cases.

3 Melt 4 tbsp / 50 g of the butter. Sift the flour and cornstarch (cornflour), baking powder and salt into a large bowl. Add the sugar and thyme.

4 Put the milk and egg into a jug. Grate in the cheese and whisk together with a fork.

5 Drain the potatoes and add to the flour mixture. Pour the liquid ingredients into the dry ingredients and stir together until just combined. Spoon the mixture equally into the greased pan or muffin cases.

6 Bake in the oven for 15–20 minutes until the muffins are firm to the touch and a toothpick (cocktail stick) inserted into the center comes out clean. Leave to cool in the pan for 3 minutes and then transfer to a wire rack and leave to cool.

7 Dice the remaining butter and serve the muffins topped with a knob of butter, garnished with watercress and some tomato salsa. Served with extra cheese.

APPLE AND CINNAMON MUFFINS

Ingredients
Makes 8

1 stick / 125 g butter, softened

Heaped ½ cup / 125 g superfine (caster) sugar

2 large eggs

1¼ cup / 125 g all purpose (plain) flour

1 tsp baking powder

½ tsp baking soda (bicarbonate of soda)

1 tsp cinnamon

3–4 oz / 100 g apple sauce

1 tsp cinnamon

For the frosting:

2 cups / 200 g confectioners' (icing) sugar

About 5 tbsp milk

1 tsp vanilla extract

½ tsp cinnamon

1 apple

2 tbsp lemon juice

Method
Prep and cook time: 40 min

1 Preheat the oven to 350°F (180°C / Gas Mark 4). Line an 8 hole muffin pan with paper muffin cases.

2 Put the butter and sugar in a large bowl and, using a hand-held electric whisk, beat together until light and fluffy.

3 Add the eggs to the mixture, one at a time, beating thoroughly after each addition.

4 Sift in the flour, baking powder, baking soda and cinnamon. Add the apple sauce and stir everything together until combined.

5 Divide the mixture equally between the muffin cases.

6 Bake in the oven for 25 minutes until firm or a toothpick (cocktail stick) inserted into the center comes out clean. Leave to cool on a wire rack.

7 To make the frosting, sift the confectioners' (icing) sugar into a large bowl. Add the milk and vanilla and mix until smooth. If the frosting is too stiff, add a little extra milk. Spoon the frosting on top of the muffins, allowing it to drizzle down the sides.

8 Quarter, core and slice the apple and toss the slices in the lemon juice. Sprinkle the cinnamon over the muffins and top with the apple pieces.

APPLE MUFFINS WITH SUNFLOWER SEEDS

Ingredients
Makes 12

4 tbsp / 50 g butter

2 apples

2¼ cups / 225 g all purpose (plain) flour

2 tsp baking powder

⅓ cup / 75 g brown sugar

1 tsp mixed spice

1 egg

⅔ cup / 150 ml sour (soured) cream

2 oz / 50 g sunflower seeds

2 tbsp raw brown (demerara) sugar, to decorate

Method
Prep and cook time: 35 min

1 Preheat the oven to 375°F (190°C / Gas Mark 5). Line a 12 hole muffin pan with paper muffin cases.

2 Melt the butter. Peel, core and finely chop the apples.

3 Sift the flour and baking powder into a large bowl. Stir in the sugar, mixed spice and apples.

4 Put the egg, sour cream and melted butter in a jug and mix together with a fork.

5 Pour the liquid ingredients into the flour mixture and stir for a few seconds until just combined.

6 Spoon the mixture into the muffin cases. Sprinkle over the sunflower seeds and the brown sugar.

7 Bake in the oven for 15–20 minutes until the muffins are well risen and firm. Leave to cool on a wire rack.

CARROT BREAD

Ingredients

3 cups / 300 g all purpose (plain) flour

1¼ cups / 125 g wholemeal flour

2 tsp baking powder

½–1 tbsp ground cinnamon

1 cup / 100 g walnuts, chopped

1 cup / 100 g desiccated coconut

10 oz / 300 g grated carrots

1⅓ cups / 300 ml light vegetable oil

1 tbsp vanilla extract

1½ cups / 300 g superfine (caster) sugar

4 large eggs, lightly beaten

Method
Prep and cook time: 55 min

1 Preheat the oven to 350°F (180°C / Gas Mark 4). Grease and line a 2 lb / 900 g loaf pan (tin).

2 Sift the all purpose (plain) flour, wholemeal flour, baking powder and ground cinnamon into a bowl.

3 Stir in the nuts, coconut and carrots.

4 Pour the oil, vanilla and sugar into a bowl and whisk together, then whisk in the eggs.

5 Add the dry ingredients to the wet ingredients. Fold everything together to combine.

6 Pour the mixture into the prepared tin. Bake for 45 minutes or until lightly browned. Insert a toothpick (cocktail stick) into the center of the bread. If it comes out clean the bread is ready.

PINEAPPLE AND CARROT MUFFINS

Ingredients

Makes 12

9 oz / 250 g carrots

2¼ cups / 225 g all purpose (plain) flour

1 tsp ground cinnamon

1 tsp mixed spice

1 tbsp baking powder

Heaped 1 cup / 225 g superfine (caster) sugar

5 oz / 150 g sweetened shredded coconut

3–4 oz /100 g raisins

2½ oz / 75 g hazelnuts, roughly chopped

7 oz / 200 g can crushed pineapple, drained

2 eggs

¾ cup / 150 ml vegetable oil

⅔ cup /150 ml sour (soured) cream

1 tsp vanilla extract

To decorate:

3 tbsp runny honey

4 tbsp sweetened shredded coconut

1 tbsp hazelnuts, roughly chopped

24 pieces dried pineapple

Method

Prep and cook time: 50 min

1 Preheat the oven to 375°F (190°C / Gas Mark 5). Line a 12 hole muffin pan (tin) with paper muffin cases.

2 Grate the carrots. Sift the flour, cinnamon, mixed spice and baking powder into a large bowl. Stir in the grated carrots, sugar, coconut, raisins, hazelnuts and pineapple.

3 Put the eggs, oil, sour cream and vanilla extract in a jug and whisk together with a fork.

4 Add the liquid ingredients to the flour mixture and stir together until just combined.

5 Divide the mixture equally between the muffin cases. Bake in the oven for 20 minutes until the muffins are risen and firm.

6 Meanwhile, warm the honey to decorate. When the muffins are cooked, brush the tops with the honey and sprinkle over the coconut and hazelnuts. Return to the oven for 5 minutes to lightly brown the coconut.

7 Dip the tips of the pineapple pieces into the runny honey and push into the top of each muffin. Leave to cool on a wire rack.

CRANBERRY BREAD

Ingredients

3 tbsp / 45g butter

1 cup / 100 g buckwheat flour

1 cup / 100 g wholemeal (whole wheat) flour

Heaped ¾ cup / 75 g ground almonds

1 tsp baking powder

½ cup / 100 g superfine (caster) sugar

¼ cup / 50 g soft brown sugar

4–5 oz / 125 g fresh or dried cranberries

2 large eggs

½ cup / 125 ml orange juice

4 tbsp natural yogurt

1 tsp grated orange zest

Method

Prep and cook time: 1 hour 20 min

1 Preheat the oven to 350°F (180°C / Gas Mark 4). Grease and flour a 2lb / 900 g loaf pan (tin).

2 Melt the butter and set aside. Put the buckwheat and wholemeal flour into a large bowl. Add the ground almonds and baking powder.

3 Add the superfine sugar, brown sugar and cranberries to the flour mixture and stir together.

4 Break the eggs into a jug and beat with a fork until frothy. Gradually stir in the orange juice, yogurt, orange zest and melted butter.

5 Pour the liquid ingredients into the flour mixture and stir to combine.

6 Pour the batter into the prepared loaf pan.

7 Bake in the oven for 1 hour until firm to the touch, or a toothpick (cocktail stick) inserted into the center comes out clean. Leave to cool on a wire rack and serve sliced.

SOYA WHOLEMEAL BREAD

Ingredients
Makes 1 large loaf

6½ cups / 650 g strong wholemeal bread flour

1 tsp salt

1 tsp sugar

2 tbsp / 25 g butter

¼ oz / 7 g easy-blend dried yeast

2 cups / 450 ml lukewarm soya milk

4 tbsp sesame seeds

Method
Prep and cook time: 1 hour plus 40 min rising time

1 Grease a baking sheet. Put the flour, salt and sugar into a large bowl. Add the butter, in small pieces, and rub the mixture together with your fingertips until the mixture forms fine crumbs.

2 Sprinkle over the dried yeast and pour in the warm soya milk. Mix together with your hands until the mixture combines to make a rough dough ball.

3 Turn the dough out on to a lightly floured surface and knead for 10 minutes until smooth and elastic.

4 Shape the dough into a round and sprinkle over the sesame seeds. Put on the prepared baking sheet.

5 Cover loosely with clear wrap (clingfilm) or a clean tea towel and leave to rise in a warm place for 30–40 minutes until doubled in size.

6 Preheat the oven to 200°C (400°F / Gas Mark 6). When the bread is well risen, remove the clear wrap and bake in the oven for about 35 minutes until golden brown. The bread is cooked when the base is tapped and it sounds hollow. Leave to cool on a wire rack.

ROSEMARY BREAD

Ingredients
Makes 1 loaf

2 eggs

1 tsp easy-blend dried yeast

4 cups / 400 g strong white bread flour

3 tbsp chopped fresh rosemary

1 tbsp superfine (caster) sugar

4 tbsp extra virgin olive oil

Method
Prep and cook time: 1 hour 10 min plus 40 min rising time

1 Grease a 2 lb / 900 g loaf pan (tin). Put the eggs into a measuring jug and whisk together with a fork. Add warm water, to make up to the volume of 10 fl oz / 275 ml.

2 Pour the liquid into a bowl, sprinkle over the yeast and add the flour, rosemary, sugar and olive oil. Bring the mixture together with your hands.

3 Turn the dough out on to a lightly floured surface and knead for 10 minutes until smooth and elastic.

4 Shape the dough into an oblong and put into the prepared loaf pan.

5 Cover loosely with plastic wrap (clingfilm) or a clean tea towel and leave to rise in a warm place for about 40 minutes until doubled in size.

6 Preheat the oven to 400°F (200°C / Gas Mark 6). Bake the bread in the oven for 45–50 minutes until golden brown. The bread is cooked when the base is tapped and it sounds hollow. Leave to cool on a wire rack.

LEMON AND POPPY SEED MUFFINS

Ingredients

Makes 12

2½ oz / 75 g poppy seeds

Finely grated zest and juice of 2 lemons

½ tsp saffron strands

½ cup / 100 ml sunflower oil

½ cup / 100 g superfine (caster) sugar

2 eggs

1 cup / 250 ml natural yogurt

3 cups / 300 g all purpose (plain) flour

2 tsp baking powder

½ tsp baking soda (bicarbonate of soda)

Method

Prep and cook time: 30 min

1 Preheat the oven to 400°F (200°C /Gas Mark 6). Generously grease a 12 hole muffin pan (tin). Sprinkle three-quarters of the poppy seeds over the base and sides of the muffin cups.

2 Put the lemon juice in a cup and add the saffron strands. Set aside.

3 Put the sunflower oil, sugar, eggs and yogurt into a jug and mix together with a fork.

4 Sift the flour, baking powder and baking soda into a large bowl. Add the lemon zest.

5 Lift the saffron threads out of the lemon juice and reserve. Pour the lemon juice into the jug of liquid ingredients, and then add the liquid to the flour mixture. Gently stir together until just combined.

6 Divide the mixture evenly between the prepared muffin cups.

7 Bake in the oven for 10–15 minutes until the muffins are risen and firm. Leave to cool on a wire rack. Sprinkle with the remaining poppy seeds and serve decorated with the reserved saffron threads.

BANANA, ZUCCHINI AND APRICOT LOAF

Ingredients

Makes 1 loaf

2¼ cups / 225 g all purpose white (plain) flour

1 tsp baking soda (bicarbonate of soda)

½ tsp cream of tartar

7 tbsp / 100 g butter, chopped into small pieces

Scant 1 cup / 175 g superfine (caster) sugar

Grated zest and juice 1 lemon

3 tbsp milk

2 bananas

3 oz / 75 g grated zucchini (courgettes)

2 oz / 50 g dried apricots, chopped

2 eggs, beaten

Method

Prep and cook time: 1 hour 30 min

1 Preheat the oven to 350°F (180°C / Gas Mark 4). Grease and line a 2 lb / 900 g loaf pan (tin).

2 Put the flour, baking soda (bicarbonate of soda) and cream of tartar in a food processor or large bowl. Add the butter and whiz to form crumbs, or rub together with your fingertips.

3 Add the sugar to the dry ingredients. Pour in the lemon zest and juice and the milk.

4 Put the bananas in a bowl and mash with a fork. Add to the bowl with the zucchini (courgettes), apricots and eggs.

5 Beat the mixture vigorously with a wooden spoon to blend the ingredients together. Spoon the mixture into the prepared loaf pan.

6 Bake in the oven for 1¼ hours until risen and golden brown. Insert a toothpick (cocktail stick) into the center of the loaf and if it comes out clean the loaf is cooked. Leave in the pan for 5 minutes then turn out and leave to cool on a wire rack.

PLUM AND ALMOND MUFFINS

Ingredients
Makes 12

Heaped ¾ cup / 175 g superfine (caster) sugar

⅔ cup / 150 ml light oil

1 egg

7 tbsp / 100 ml milk

1 tsp almond extract

2 cups / 200 g all purpose (plain) flour

1 tbsp baking powder

½ cup / 75 g ground almonds

7 oz / 200 g plums, quartered and stoned

Method
Prep and cook time: 35 min

1 Preheat the oven to 375°F (190°C / Gas Mark 5). Line a 12 hole muffin pan (tin) with paper muffin cases or generously grease the cups.

2 Put the sugar, oil, egg, milk and almond extract in a jug and mix together with a fork.

3 Sift the flour and baking powder into a large bowl. Add the ground almonds and mix together.

4 Add the plums to the flour mixture and toss together to coat the plums in the flour.

5 Add the liquid ingredients to the flour mixture and stir together until just combined.

6 Spoon the mixture evenly between the muffin cases or prepared cups.

7 Bake in the oven for 15–20 minutes until the muffins are pale golden brown, risen and firm. Leave to cool on a wire rack.

OAT AND RAISIN BREAD

Ingredients
Makes 1 loaf

3 cups / 300 g strong white bread flour

2 cups / 200 g strong wholemeal bread flour

1 cup / 150 g medium oatmeal

2 tsp salt

4 tbsp / 50 g butter

¼ oz / 7 g easy-blend dried yeast

3 tbsp runny honey

²/₃ cups / 150 ml natural yogurt

1¼ cups / 300 ml warm water

Heaped ¼ cup / 50 g raisins

Method
Prep and cook time: 50 min plus 40 min rising time

1 Grease a 2 lb / 900 g loaf pan (tin). Put the white and wholemeal flour, the oatmeal, salt and the butter, cut into small pieces, into a large bowl. Sprinkle over the dried yeast.

2 Pour in the honey, yogurt and warm water into the dry ingredients and mix together with your hands until the mixture forms a rough ball.

3 Turn the dough out on to a lightly floured surface and knead for 10 minutes until smooth and elastic. Knead in the raisins.

4 Shape the dough into an oblong and put into the prepared loaf pan.

5 Cover loosely with plastic wrap (clingfilm) or a clean tea towel and leave to rise in a warm place for 30–40 minutes until doubled in size.

6 Preheat the oven to 400°F (200°C / Gas Mark 6). Bake the bread in the oven for 35 minutes until golden brown. The bread is cooked when the base is tapped and it sounds hollow. Leave to cool on a wire rack.

APPLE SCONES

Ingredients

Makes 8

2¼ cups / 225 g all purpose (plain) flour

2 tsp baking powder

1 tsp baking soda (bicarbonate of soda)

Pinch of salt

3 tbsp superfine (caster) sugar

4 tbsp / 50 g butter

1 apple

1 egg

⅓ cup / 75 ml milk, plus extra to glaze

Method

Prep and cook time: 30 min

1 Preheat the oven to 450°F (230°C / Gas Mark 8). Place an ungreased baking sheet in the oven to heat.

2 Sift the flour, baking powder, baking soda, salt and add 2 tbsp of the sugar into a large bowl.

3 Cut the butter into cubes, add to the flour mixture and rub in with your fingertips until the mixture forms crumbs.

4 Peel, core and finely chop the apple. Add to the dry ingredients and stir to coat in the the apple in the flour mixture.

5 Put the egg and milk in a jug and mix together with a fork. Gradually pour into the flour mixture and bring the everything together with your hands to make a soft, manageable dough.

6 Roll out the dough on a lightly floured surface to ¾ inch / 2 cm thickness. Using a 2 inch / 5 cm plain cutter, stamp out 8 rounds.

7 Use a palette knife to lift the scones on to the preheated baking sheet. Brush with milk and sprinkle with the remaining sugar.

8 Bake in the oven for 8–10 minutes until well risen, firm and pale golden. Leave to cool on a wire rack.

WALNUT AND RAISIN LOAF

Ingredients
Makes 1 loaf

4 cups / 400 g strong wholemeal bread flour

2½ cups / 250 g strong white bread flour

1 cup / 100 g chopped walnuts

2 tbsp brown sugar

1½ tsp salt

¼ oz / 7 g easy-blend dried yeast

3 tbsp walnut or sunflower oil

2 cups / 450 ml lukewarm water

⅓ cup / 75 g raisins

Method
Prep and cook time: 50 min plus 40 min rising

1 Grease a 2 lb / 900 g loaf pan (tin). Put the wholemeal and white flour, the walnuts, sugar and salt into a large bowl. Sprinkle over the dried yeast.

2 Pour the oil and warm water into the dry ingredients and mix together with your hands until the mixture forms a rough ball.

3 Turn the dough out on to a lightly floured surface and knead for 10 minutes until smooth and elastic. Knead in the raisins.

4 Shape the dough into an oblong and put into the prepared loaf pan.

5 Cover loosely with plastic wrap (clingfilm) or a clean tea towel and leave to rise in a warm place for 30–40 minutes until doubled in size.

6 Preheat the oven to 400°F (200°C / Gas Mark 6). Bake the bread in the oven for 35 minutes until golden brown. The bread is cooked when the base is tapped and it sounds hollow. Leave to cool on a wire rack.

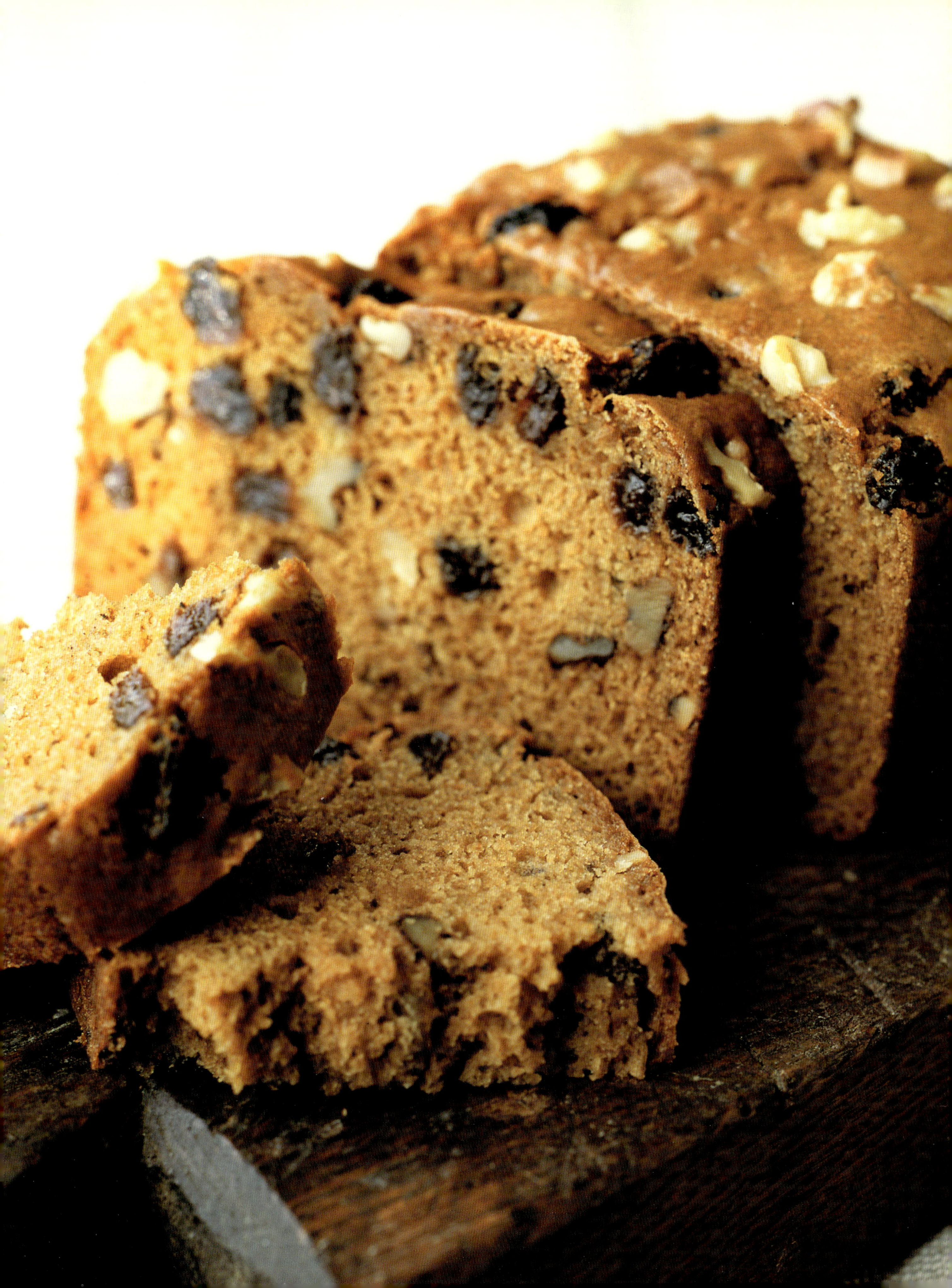

CRANBERRY ROCK CAKES

Ingredients

Makes 8

2¼ cups / 225 g all purpose (plain) flour

7 tbsp / 100 g butter

2 oz / 50 g dried cranberries

Finely grated zest of 1 orange

¼ cup / 50 g soft brown sugar

1 large egg

1 tsp baking powder

1 tsp ground cinnamon

1 tsp milk

Method

Prep and cook time: 25 min

1 Preheat the oven to 350°F (180°C / Gas Mark 4). Lightly grease a baking sheet.

2 Put the flour into a food processor or large bowl. Add the butter in small pieces and whiz to form crumbs, or rub together with your fingertips.

3 Add the cranberries, orange zest, sugar, egg, baking powder, cinnamon and milk to the flour mixture. Stir together and mix well to make a soft dough.

4 Divide the dough into 8 even-sized pieces and shape each piece into a rough mound. Put on the prepared the baking sheet.

5 Bake in the oven for 10–15 minutes until pale golden brown. Leave to cool on a wire rack.

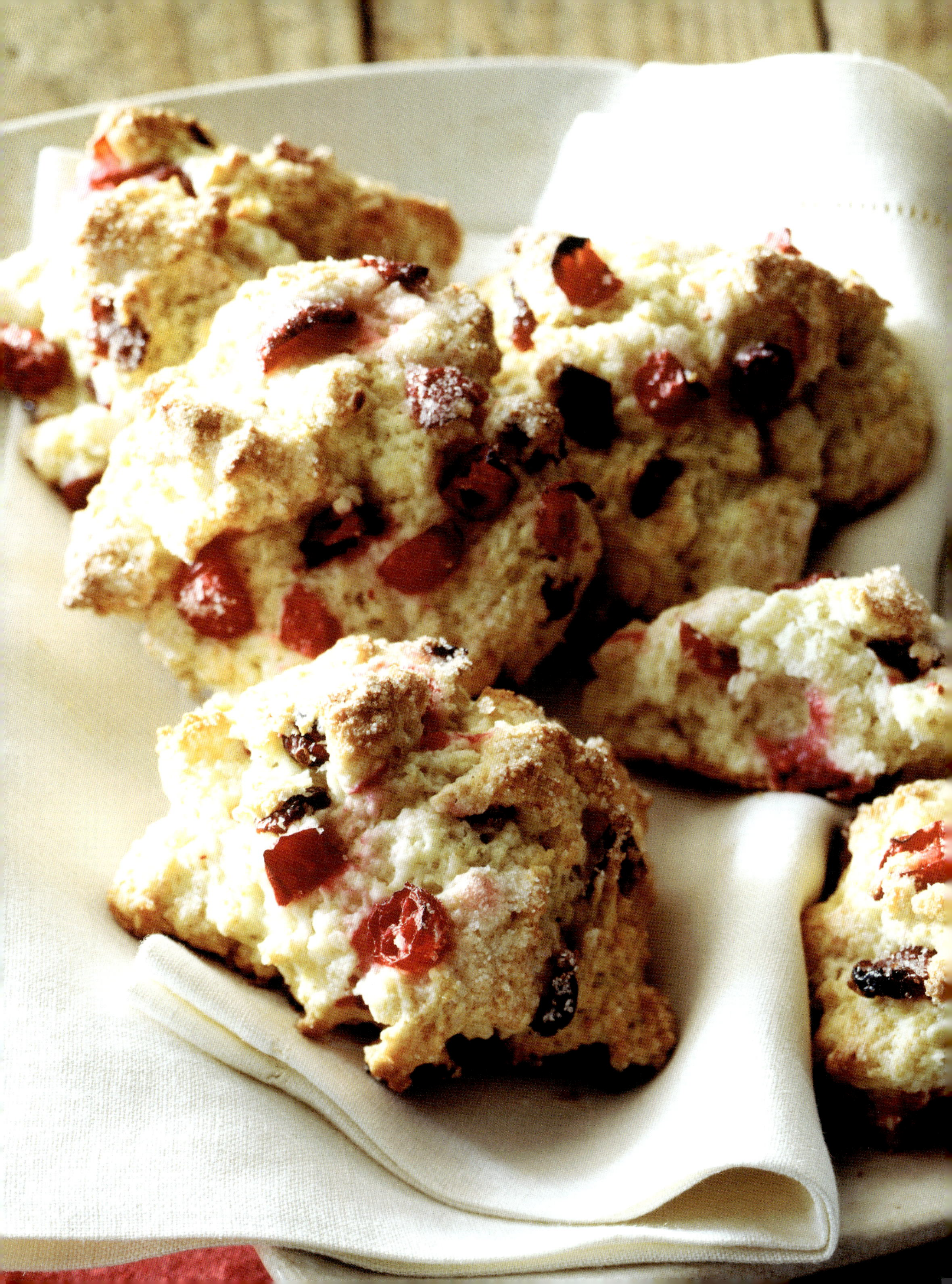

BANANA AND RAISIN MUFFINS

Ingredients
Makes 12

2 cups / 200 g wholemeal (whole wheat) flour

1 cup / 50 g bran

3 tbsp soft brown sugar

2 tsp baking powder

Heaped ½ cup / 100 g raisins

2/3 cup / 150 ml milk

1 large egg

1/3 cup / 75 ml sunflower oil

2 ripe bananas

Method
Prep and cook time: 35 min

1 Preheat the oven to 400°F (200°C / Gas Mark 6). Line a 12 hole muffin pan with paper muffin cases.

2 Put the flour, bran, sugar, baking powder and raisins in a large bowl and mix together.

3 Put the milk, egg and sunflower oil in a jug and lightly whisk together with a fork.

4 Pour the liquid ingredients into the flour mixture and stir gently together until just combined.

5 Put the bananas in a bowl and mash with a fork. Gently stir into the muffin mixture.

6 Divide the mixture evenly between the muffin cases.

7 Bake in the oven for 20–25 minutes until the muffins are firm or a toothpick (cocktail stick) inserted into the center comes out clean. Leave to cool on a wire rack.

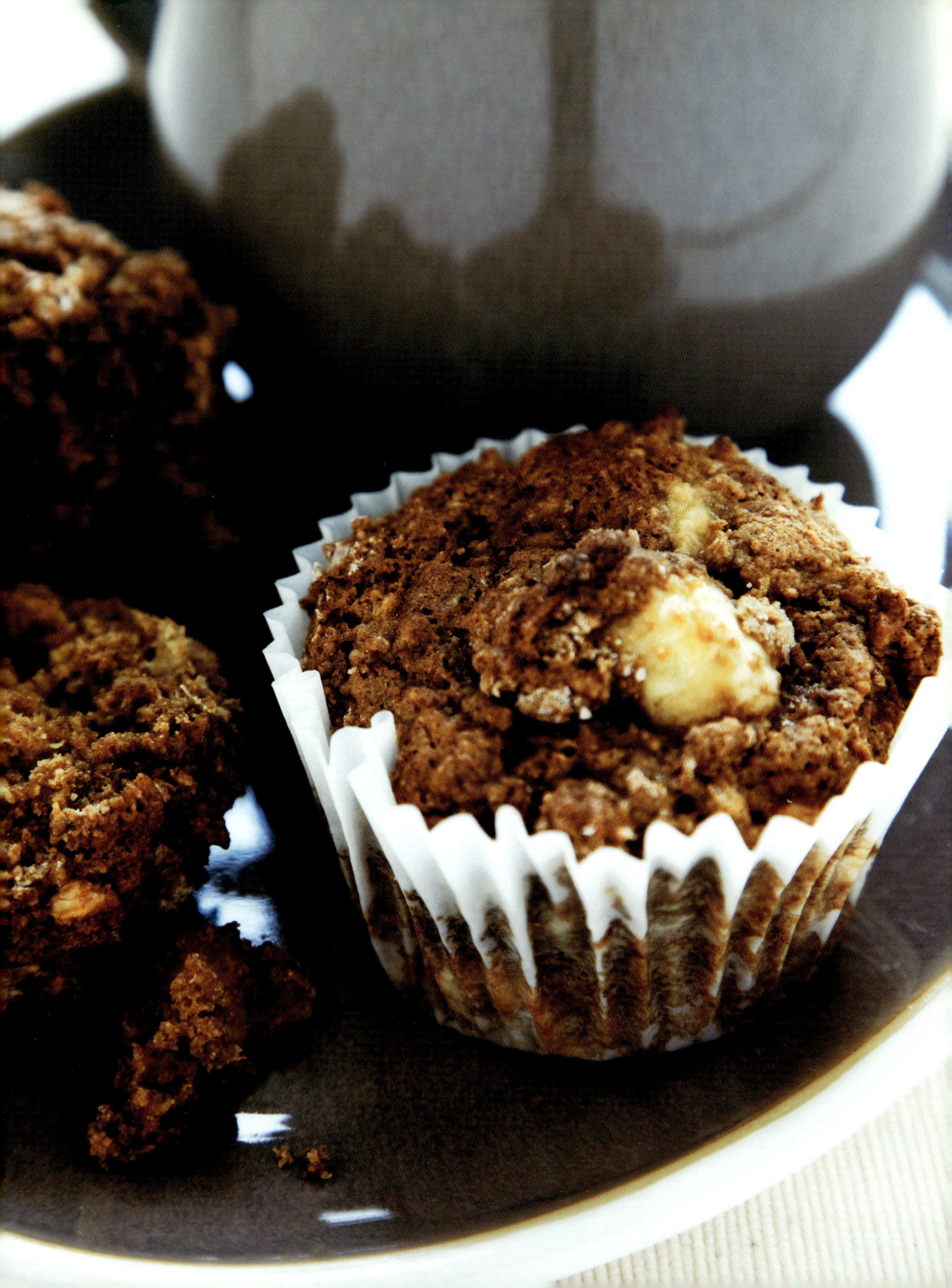

SODA BREAD

Ingredients

Makes 1 loaf

3½ cups / 350 g wholemeal flour

2 tsp baking soda (bicarbonate of soda)

1 tsp salt

1 cup / 125 g coarse oatmeal

1 tsp runny honey

1⅓ cups / 300 ml buttermilk

About 3 tbsp milk

Method

Prep and cook time: 50 min

1 Preheat the oven to 400°F (200°C / Gas Mark 6). Grease a baking sheet.

2 Sift the flour, baking soda and salt into a large bowl. Stir in the oatmeal.

3 Add the honey, buttermilk and enough milk to form a soft dough.

4 Turn the dough out on to a lightly floured surface and knead for 5 minutes until smooth and elastic.

5 Shape the dough into an 8 inch / 20 cm round and put on the prepared baking sheet. Cut a deep cross into the center of the dough and brush with a little milk.

6 Bake in the oven for 30–35 minutes until the bread is risen and firm to the touch. The bread is cooked when the base is tapped and it sounds hollow. Leave to cool on a wire rack.

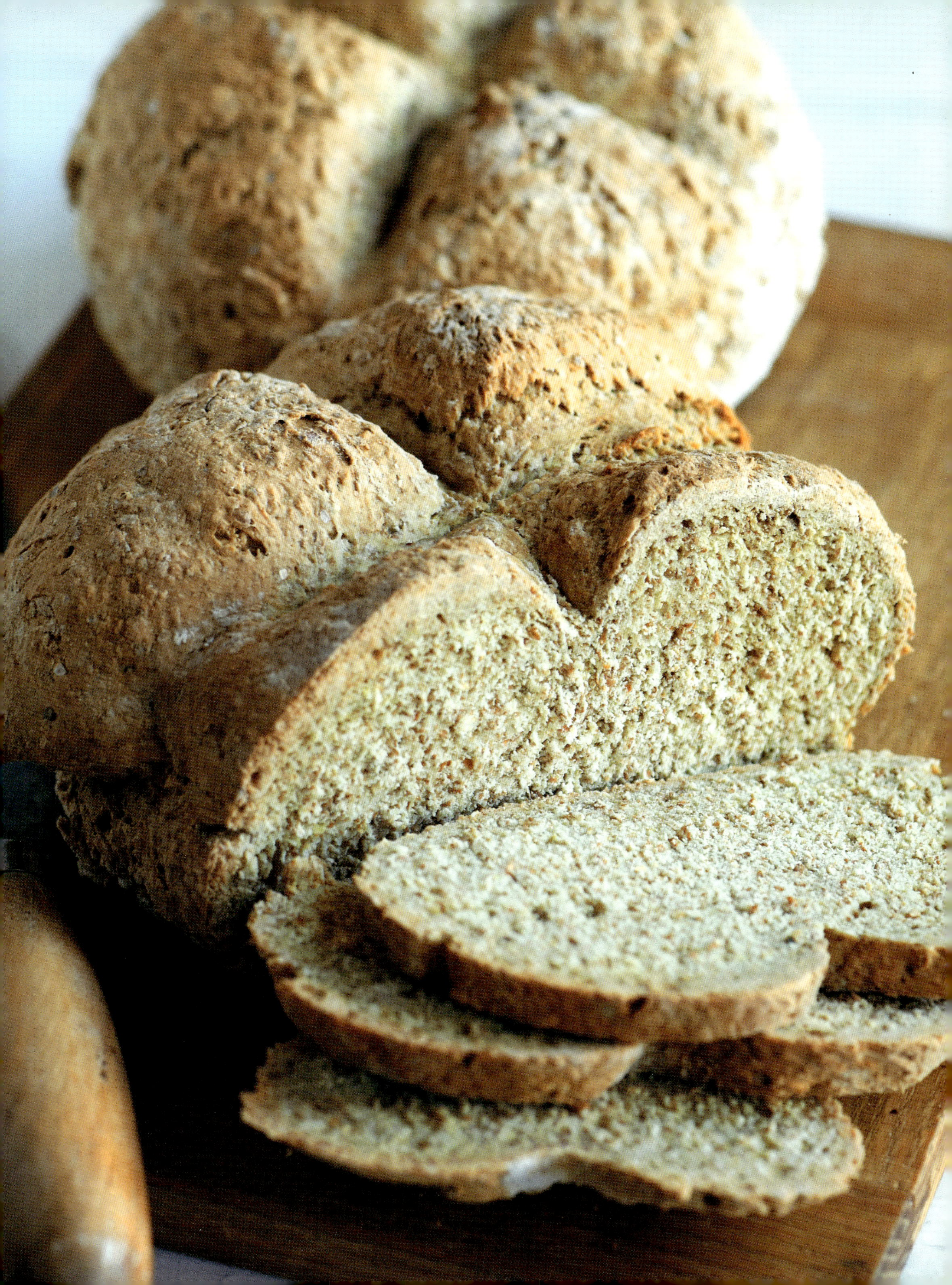

BLUEBERRY MUFFINS

Ingredients

Makes 12

4 tbsp / 50 g butter

1 egg

3 tbsp honey

Scant ½ cup / 100 ml plain yogurt

Scant ½ cup / 100 ml sour cream

2½ cups / 250 g all-purpose (plain) flour

2 tsp baking powder

2½ cups / 250 g blueberries

Confectioners' (icing) sugar, for dusting

Method

Prep and cook time: 40 min

1 Preheat the oven to 350°F (180°C / Gas Mark 4). Line a 12 hole muffin pan (tin) with paper cases. Melt the butter and leave to cool slightly, so that it is still liquid.

2 Put the egg, honey, yogurt and sour cream in a large bowl and mix together. Stir in the melted butter. Sift in the flour and baking powder and mix together. Fold in the blueberries. Fill the muffin cups three-quarters full with the batter.

3 Bake in the oven for 25–30 minutes, until golden brown. Leave to rest in the pan for 5 minutes, and then remove from the pan and leave to cool on a wire rack. Serve dusted with confectioners' (icing) sugar.

PARMESAN AND POLENTA MUFFINS

Ingredients
Makes 9

1½ cups / 150 g all purpose (plain) flour

1 tbsp baking powder

1 tsp salt

1¼ cups / 150 g yellow cornmeal (polenta)

2 tsp superfine (caster) sugar

2 tsp ground black pepper

Scant ½ cup / 50 g grated Parmesan cheese

1 cup / 225 ml milk

2 eggs, lightly beaten

4 tbsp light olive oil

Method
Prep and cook time: 30 min

1 Preheat the oven to 425°F (220°C / Gas Mark 7). Grease a 9 hole muffin pan or line with paper muffin cases.

2 Sift the flour, baking powder and salt into a large bowl. Add the cornmeal (polenta), sugar, black pepper and half of the Parmesan cheese.

3 Put the milk, eggs and olive oil in a jug and whisk together with a fork. Pour the liquid ingredients into the dry ingredients and gently stir together.

4 Divide the mixture equally between the greased pan or muffin cases. Sprinkle over the remaining Parmesan cheese.

5 Bake in the oven for 15 minutes until the muffins are well risen and firm to the touch. Leave to cool on a wire rack.

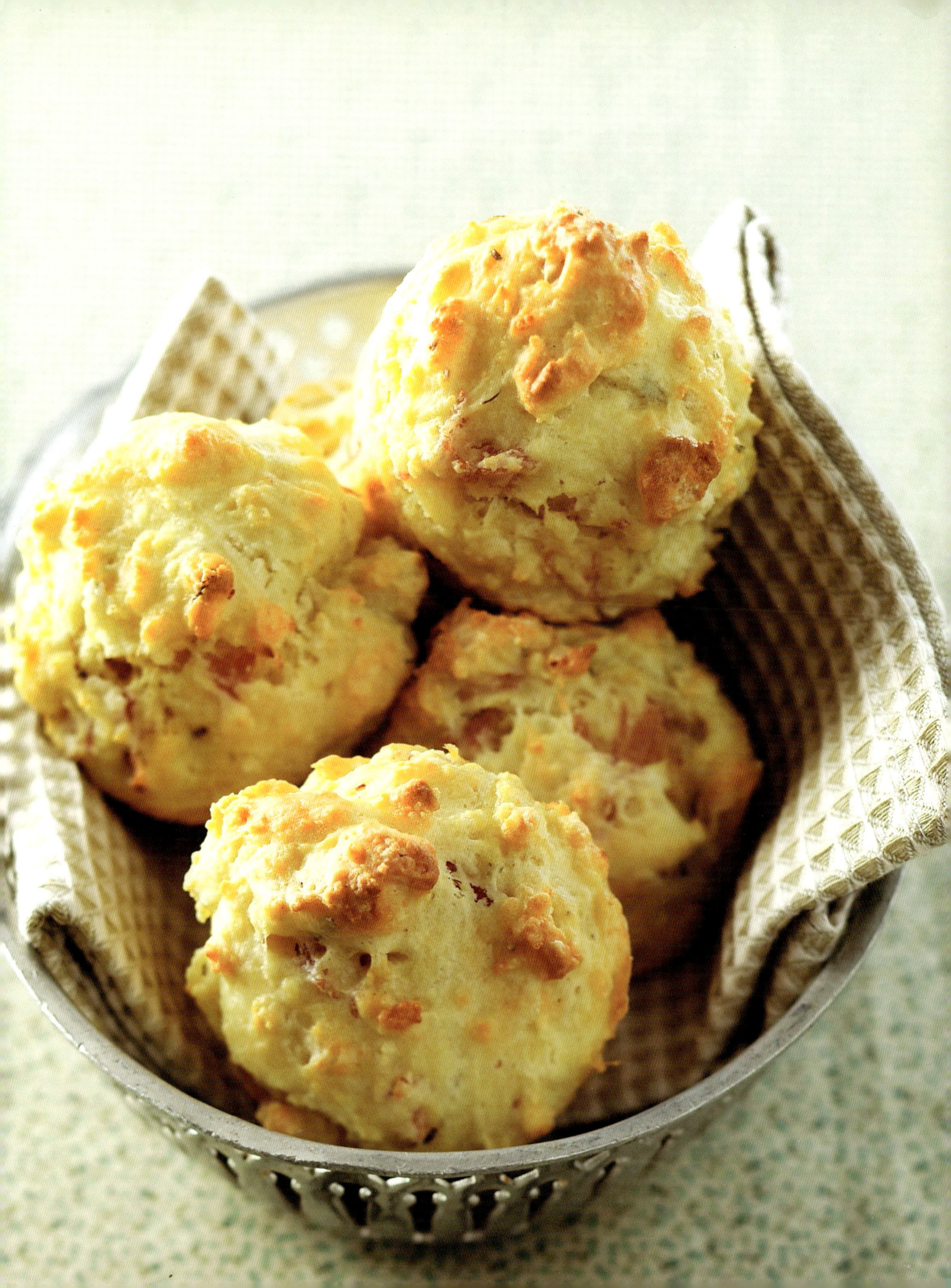

Published by Transatlantic Press

First published in 2010

Transatlantic Press
38 Copthorne Road, Croxley Green, Hertfordshire WD3 4AQ

© Transatlantic Press

Images and Recipes by StockFood © The Food Image Agency

Recipes selected by Jonnie Léger, StockFood

All rights reserved.

No part of this publication may be reproduced or transmitted in any form or by any means, electronic or mechanical, including photocopying, recording,or any information storage and retrieval system, without permission in writing from the copyright holders.

A catalogue record for this book is available from the British Library.

ISBN 978-1-908533-50-0

Printed in China